A Parent's Guide to the Santa Reveal

ISBN 979-8-89112-580-3 (Paperback)
ISBN 979-8-89112-582-7 (Hardcover)
ISBN 979-8-89112-581-0 (Digital)

Copyright © 2024 Darby Holmes
All rights reserved
First Edition

All rights reserved. No part of this publication may be reproduced, distributed, or transmitted in any form or by any means, including photocopying, recording, or other electronic or mechanical methods without the prior written permission of the publisher. For permission requests, solicit the publisher via the address below.

Covenant Books
11661 Hwy 707
Murrells Inlet, SC 29576
www.covenantbooks.com

A Parent's Guide to the Santa Reveal
Unwrapping the Magic of Christmas

Written & Illustrated by
DARBY HOLMES

Introduction

Parental warning

Dear Parent or Guardian,

Before you turn the page, I want to ensure that you are aware of the content within this book. This book is meant to reveal the truth about Saint Nicholas and Christmas traditions surrounding the legends that came from his service.

Only proceed if you are comfortable with your child hearing this information. I wrote this book for children age eight because that is when I chose to tell my children, but as a parent or guardian, you are the best judge of your child's emotional readiness.

If you choose to continue, I hope that this book will lead to meaningful discussions and an even more magical holiday season for your family.

With warm wishes,
Darby Holmes

Hello there! I'm Bella, and I've heard you've been getting pretty curious lately. Well, guess what? When you turn the age of eight, something amazing happens! It's a special age because that's when Heavenly Father says we're ready to take on more responsibilities and start uncovering the truth about the world around us.

Whether you've recently turned eight or are a bit older like me, that's perfectly fine. Heavenly Father says that we can know the truth about all things!

Do you know the truth about all things?

Well, I don't know everything either, but I am here to tell you about one truth I know.

And it's about…

CHRISTMAS!

It is so magical, but you already know that part! But do you know what makes it so magical?

I used to think it was Santa Claus and getting presents, but then I learned the truth.

Are you ready to learn the truth? Turn the page if you feel ready.

You see, there's something truly special about Christmas, and it's not because there is one person who does it all. Nope, there's actually no sleigh that flies or reindeer in the sky. The truth is, there is no Santa at all.

Now I know this might surprise you a little bit at first, but don't worry! I'm here to share with you where the real enchantment of Christmas comes from, and it's even more amazing than you can imagine!

The real magic of Christmas comes from…

YOU!

That's right! Now that you know the truth. It's up to you, me, and everyone else who knows the truth to keep the magic of Christmas going!

Keeping the Christmas magic alive is easy! While Christmas isn't just about gifts, they are a special part of it.

At the very first Christmas, the Wise Men followed the star and brought gifts to Baby Jesus, the newborn King. We put gifts at the foot of the Christmas tree to remind us of these gifts placed at the foot of Jesus long ago.

When we use the secret of Santa to give gifts, it means we give without expecting anything in return. This makes Christmas special for everyone, as millions of people around the world remember the gifts of Jesus, think of others, and give in secret, showing true selflessness.

Remember to keep Santa's secret by not telling others! Their parents will want to tell them when the time is right for them!

But there is even more to the story of Christmas and the secret of Santa.

A few hundred years after Jesus was born, His teachings and spirit inspired one man named Nicholas who noticed that some families were too poor to give gifts to their children. He decided to be Christlike and make gifts for these children and take them to their homes!

He was sneaky and gave these gifts in secret. He did this for many years until he was too old to deliver presents.

His spirit of generosity and love touched many hearts. People even made up songs about his white beard and the sleigh full of gifts he used to deliver this Christlike service. The spirit of gift-giving by Saint Nicholas became the spirit of Santa Claus.

Today, people and parents all over the world wrap presents and give them to their children in the name of Santa Claus.

Some people deliver presents to those in need as well. Saint Nicholas has helped teach others to love one another as Jesus did.

That is what makes Christmas so magical! Jesus inspired a good man to be giving, and that inspired people all over the world to continue to be giving for thousands of years during Christmas time!

To me, that is even more magical than one person doing it all by himself in one night!

I'm a kid, just like you, and I love helping make Christmas special. My parents even let me wrap some of the presents!

Now that you know the truth, that Santa Claus is actually people all over the world following the spirit of Christ, you can be a part of this beautiful tradition that brings love and joy to so many hearts during the Christmas season.

Have fun and always remember to be Christlike. This is the magic of Christmas!

Ideas for parents

Discovering that Santa Claus isn't real can be a sensitive and emotional moment for a child. Parents should approach this conversation with care and empathy. Here are some follow-up questions and statements parents can use to support their child emotionally:

1. It's okay to feel mixed emotions or even be sad. Can you tell me what's on your mind?
2. Do you have any questions about Santa or anything else you want to talk about?
3. How can we continue to spread love and generosity during this season?
4. Remember, Christmas is still a special time for us to be together as a family. What are some of your favorite holiday traditions?
5. Is there anything else you'd like to know or discuss about Christmas or our family traditions?
6. Is there anything else on your mind that you'd like to discuss?

Remember to be patient, understanding, and reassuring during this conversation. Children may have a range of emotions, so make sure they know that their feelings are valid and that Christmas remains a special time for your family to come together and celebrate love and faith.

Ideas for keeping the magic alive for older children

Here are some wonderful traditions that families have embraced to maintain the magic of Christmas even after Santa's secret has been revealed.

1. Santa's Little Helpers: Allow the older child or children to become Santa's little helpers. They can take part in wrapping presents or creatively arranging gifts for a magical Christmas morning surprise. This will warm their hearts when they see their little siblings' eyes light up on Christmas morning!
2. Cookie Crumbs: Let the older child or children nibble on some of the cookies and milk left out for Santa. Be sure to leave behind just a few crumbs and a sip of milk for the younger siblings to discover!
3. Stocking Surprise: Let the older child or children pick out a special gift to secretly place in the stockings of their younger siblings.
4. Jingle All the Way: Give your older child or children some jingle bells and send them outside to jingle them outside the younger child or children's window without being seen. They may see the littles rush to the window and gaze up at the starry skies.
5. Sibling Elves: Older siblings become a Santa's elf for their younger siblings. They pick an elf name and leave notes around the house in December, mentioning good deeds or kindness observed. It is a fun way for older kids to serve and celebrate their younger siblings at Christmas.

These traditions not only help maintain the magic of Christmas but also strengthen the bonds between siblings and instill a sense of giving, kindness, and joy of keeping the spirit of Santa Claus alive in the hearts of your children.

About the Author

Darby is a mother and graphic designer. She loves family history work and is always trying to brainstorm innovative ways to help others feel connected to their family and Christ through storybooks, games, and art. When she's not conjuring up these projects, she enjoys talking up a storm whitewater rafting or belting out a tune. When it's time to unwind, she is giddy to snuggle with her hubby, watching a show and savoring a delightful spread of cheese and crackers.

Printed in the USA
CPSIA information can be obtained
at www.ICGtesting.com
LVHW062032261124
797345LV00020B/452